S0-CCF-376

Embracing Your Power in 30 Days

A Journey of Self-Discovery and Personal Freedom

Copyright © July 2005
by Wanda Marie and Yolanda King

All Rights Reserved.

For information about permission to reproduce selections
from this book, write to:
Wanda Marie
12404 Sanford Street
Los Angeles, California 90066
1-310-827-4166 ~ info@wandamarie.com

ISBN: 0-9771653-0-2

A Special Thanks to:

Ron Stacker Thompson
Ron Lapointe
Philip Osburn Mott
Tanya White

for their loving guidance,
feedback and support of this project.

Contents

*Each Number Represents a Step Closer
to Self-Discovery and Personal Freedom*

Introduction

Once upon a time in a land very very close to home, there was this little frog named "Wimpy Wanna" who just walked. He did not jump or leap as frogs are designed to do, but just walked along, wondering why life was so awkward for him. He whined and complained about life continuously.

And then one day, out of the blue and through the law of grace, there appeared another frog that looked just like him. But this frog was jumping all over the place and leaping and hopping and clearly having a ball! So Wimpy Wanna asked the zealous frog. "How do you do this jumping around and leaping thing?" The zealous frog said simply, "I know who and what I am. I am a frog just like you. We are supposed to jump and leap and have fun! Be yourself, stop holding back—lets go!" The zealous frog led the way and one step at a time Wimpy Wanna learned how to be himself. He embraced his own power and used it to leap and jump through life just as he was designed to do, just as all of us are designed to do.

Greetings, and welcome to a 30-day transformational journey that will change your life if you allow it. Too many of us go through life wimpy because we wanna be, do and have more than what is showing up for us, yet we don't always know why or where to start. In my willingness to change and grow, my search led me to a dear friend and Life Coach, Wanda Marie, who has often been my zealous frog. I have invited Wanda to participate in the writing of this book so that together through my personal commentary and her inspirational exercises as tools for change, this book may become your zealous frog, showing you the path to embracing your power, becoming more of yourself, free to do all of the things in life you were designed to do.

So let's start with why embracing your power is so important. Developing and strengthening your own potential allows you to more effectively contribute to the betterment of wherever you find yourself. Living your best life reverberates and makes a difference in your family relationships, your love life, your workplace, your community and ultimately on our planet. You do make a difference.

As we begin, lets define what we mean by personal power. For me, personal power shows up as a demonstration of healthy self-love. It comes from the inside out, a sense of inner power, empowerment. It is not looking for validation outside of yourself. It is knowing that all that you need is within you. What it really boils down to is a commitment to love yourself. Yes, I'm talking about self-love. Some people may think of that as being selfish, but it isn't. Selfish love is an egotistical, better-than-anybody-else, boastful love of superficial things, such as the way you look, the way you dress, what you have, where you've been. That isn't self-love. That is an ego-based life that is often filled with lots of drama and very little peace and no real sense of self or true personal empowerment.

Self-love, on the other hand, recognizes and appreciates your inner attributes, your confidence, bravery, compassion, your sense of responsibility. Self-love recognizes your sense of humor, loyalty, trustworthiness, and integrity. You are a unique original, a divine original. Interestingly enough, when you learn to love yourself, not judged against external standards, but by taking inventory of all the good that already exists within you, you also learn how to really love others. Because no matter what we may see in the popular culture, you really can't love anyone else until you can truly love yourself. You just can't give unless you've developed something to offer.

Building self-love and self-esteem does not happen over night, it is an ongoing journey. I am convinced that much of the unhappiness in the world is caused by people who don't love themselves enough.

It takes courage to love yourself, to be able to look yourself square in the eyes and say "I love you just the way you are." It takes courage to trust your gut instincts when logic tells you differently. It takes courage to say "no" to a friend or loved one in need when you know you must honor yourself by saying "no." It takes courage to stay free when everyone around you is in pain. It takes courage to know your own truth when the truth of the majority appears to be different. It takes courage to be authentically you, and it takes all the personal power you can muster up to be yourself and absolutely free. Sometimes life becomes so difficult that not being true to yourself becomes more painful than you can handle, so you surrender and let go and self-love begins to surface.

Because of the legacy I was born into, for too long I was bogged down in other people's expectations of who and what I should be. For years, I tried to deny the voice inside in order to please the voices outside. And in my case, which I suspect isn't too different from yours, there was a rousing chorus of voices, each with a different pitch, often singing different verses. How could I be so many things to so many people? It was a recipe for self-doubt, self-denial, a feeling of failure.

What became clear is that I was going to have to find a quiet place away from the chorus, and listen to that still small inner voice that had been urging me for so long to take that journey toward self-love. I've come a long way—have had a few setbacks, had to refocus a few times. But I am a witness to the fact that self-love brings peace, happiness and excellence into your life.

Wanda and I have identified eight areas of self concern that we feel must be addressed in order to love yourself enough to embrace your power and live the magnificent life you were born to live:

- Self-Awareness (facing your true self)
- Self-Acceptance (honoring who you are)
- Self-Love (learning self-care)
- Self-Discipline (willingness to grow)
- Self-Confidence (knowing you are enough)
- Self-Expression (expressing your magnificence)
- Self-Appreciation (embracing your power)
- Self-Mastery (living in the love)

This 30-day journey of self-discovery and personal freedom will walk you through each of these areas of self-concern, offering you one step each day that will take you along the path of loving yourself, embracing your power and living your life more fully. The best way to utilize this book is to set aside a specific time each morning and at night for your daily transformation work. We are suggesting first thing in the morning allowing it to set the tone for your day, and the last thing at night allowing it to permeate your mind as you drift off into dream state each night. And please don't beat yourself up if you miss a day. Just love yourself enough to pick up from where you left off and, by all means, keep going.

Each morning, we will offer you a little **commentary** about the step for the day to help you to better understand it, and then you will be led through an **exercise** to help you to embrace it. Once you have completed the exercise, which may not be until the end of the day, we ask that you **journal** any thoughts, feelings, ideas or insights received during the exercise. Journaling causes you to stop and focus, to be present with your thoughts and feelings. It helps you to sort things out more clearly. Another reason I personally want you to keep a journal is because so many times along the way I would forget how far I'd come when the journey seemed impossible. However, when I could look back and see my gains, it provided the needed strength to keep moving forward. I didn't keep a journal in the beginning so my search for how far I'd come often took some time to figure out. I want you to keep a journal so that when you need to know your progress, it's right there for you and your moving forward will not be delayed by a search into the past.

It is possible that the exercise may stir up some uncomfortable feelings, so we offer a **positive affirmation** for each step as a tool for handling any negative mind chatter that would limit your moving forward on the path. Even if there is no negative mind chatter around the step, we encourage you to utilize the affirmation as a tool for taking you to the next level of your journey even faster. Try to commit the affirmation to memory so that you may silently recite it to yourself throughout the day to bombard your mind with positive thoughts. Finally, you will be asked to **visualize** something meaningful, such as your best life as you drift off to sleep each night. Visualization is a powerful tool. It trains your mind to see the impossible as though it is possible. If you can see it, you can indeed achieve it. Begin to see the life you want to create for yourself. And, by all means, dream big!

There are no guarantees in life. However, we do believe that if you follow the path outlined in this book and stick to it, your life will dramatically change for the better in 30 days or less.

Once you have completed this book, know that your journey is really just beginning. Take the time to work the book again and again until each exercise in the book becomes such a part of who you are, that you no longer have to think about it. It just happens naturally through you, and as you. Lets begin.

Self-Awareness
Steps 1 through 4

Facing Your True Self

*This first part deals with getting clear
on who you are and what you want.*

*In order to begin the process of embracing
your power you must begin with you.*

DAY 1
SELF-AWARENESS

Who Am I Really?

Commentary

In 1971, in Atlanta, Georgia, I was on stage before God and everybody playing the role of a prostitute and kissing a White man. That's right, Dr. King's first born daughter, only 15 years old at the time. Not only were segments of the over-all community up in arms, but our religious community was appalled. I was so excited to be cast in the play, *"The Owl and the Pussycat,"* my very first professional production. I never knew it would cause such controversy. This really tested my resolve to be an actor. More importantly, it was my wake-up call to myself that rang out loud and clear, "This is who I am." Though my heart was beating like a jackhammer before every performance because I was so worried about the comments of my family and community, everything inside of me still had to get on that stage and perform.

When I was a little girl, my father tried to discourage me from becoming an actor as he didn't think it was a wise choice. My father was my first buddy and we shared such a loving connection, that going against his wishes really affected my confidence, and it was very difficult for me to ignore what he felt. Yet, I had to be true to myself. I am someone who needs to express myself through acting. Being an actor and an artist of communication is, and will always be, the way my soul sings. What makes your soul sing? Who are you, really?

Exercise

Close your eyes and think back to when you were a child and ask yourself these questions.

- What did I dream of becoming when I grew up?
- What games did I enjoy playing the most?
- What toys brought me the greatest joy?
- What motivates me today?

Just allow yourself to be with these thoughts throughout the day. There is nothing in particular you have to do with them; simply contemplate them. Do not judge your answers or your progress in life; simply ponder each question and your response.

Affirmation

Commit the following positive affirmation to memory and silently recite it to yourself throughout the day whenever you think of it, or to counter any negative feelings or emotions that may surface as you contemplate today's questions and your answers.

I am Divinity expressing life fully.

Visualization

Let this be the last thing you do before you drift off to sleep. If you pray and/or meditate at night, do these activities prior to your visualization process. Visualization is a powerful tool for manifestation. If you can see it you can achieve it. Those without vision perish. The imagination of a child is what is missing in the lives of many adults. Learn to imagine once again, imagine a world that you create as perfect for you, imagine your best life possible as you drift off to sleep. See yourself being, doing and having everything your heart desires right now—feel it and make it real with the power of your mind. Make it real and take that essence with you into your sleep state so that your subconscious mind has something wonderful to work on as you sleep.

Journal

You may use this space or your own journal to write down any thoughts, feelings, ideas or insights that may have come up for you during the exercise.

DAY 2
SELF-AWARENESS

What Do I Really Want in Life?

Commentary

Well, I thought I wanted to be a star. As it turns out, what I really wanted, was to make a difference. I had to be clear about what I really wanted in life because being an actor alone didn't seem significant in comparison with the path of peace and freedom my family was pursuing. So, I allowed other people's opinions to dictate the value of my own desires. This prevented me from putting all my heart and soul into what I wanted to do with my life, causing me to feel lost and confused. Being distracted by other people's opinions caused me to be pulled in different directions and taken off my path. Later in life, as I began to embrace my power, I realized that I didn't have to choose. I could make a difference in the world and do it from center stage.

Taking a really close look at who you are sets the foundation for what you really want in life. I believe we have two desires, the desires of our soul and the desires of our ego. My ego really wanted to be on stage. My soul really wanted to make a difference in the world. Knowing that this is what I truly wanted in life, I became an actor on a mission; a mission to help bring more peace to the planet. What a blessing it is to know what you really want from life and be empowered enough to pursue it. Do you know what you really want from life?

Exercise

Ponder the following questions. Within your answers, see if there is a common thread that reveals to you what you really want from life.

If your life were absolutely perfect what would it look like:

- Physically (where would you live, what car would you drive, how would you dress)
- Mentally (what would your creative expression be in the world)
- Emotionally (how would you be expressing your joy and happiness)
- Spiritually (what would your beliefs be about God)

If money were no object, how would you spend your life?

How would you spend your time if you did not need to work for money?

Affirmation

Commit the following positive affirmation to memory, and silently recite it to yourself throughout the day whenever you think of it, or to counter any negative thoughts, or to simply reinforce the idea that anything is possible in an abundant universe.

I know who I am, and
my purpose reveals itself clearly.

Visualization

Read the questions for today once again just prior to sleep but this time do not ponder any answers. As you drift off to sleep tonight, imagine that you have a Spirit Guide who has come to you and said "Last night as you went to sleep, you visualized what your best life would look like. Now allow me to show you what I see for you, as your best life." And then open your mind and allow your imagination to show you an even bigger vision for your life, accepting no limitations, being free enough to dream big. Let go now as you drift off into a deep, relaxing, and peaceful sleep.

Journal

You may use this space or your own journal to write down any thoughts, feelings, ideas or insights that may have come up for you during the exercise.

DAY 3
SELF-AWARENESS

What's Holding Me Back?

Commentary

One of my greatest fears was speaking my truth and becoming too successful for it. My father spoke his truth and became very successful at it, and look what happened to him. My role model for speaking up paid a very high price for his voice. So my fear kept me quiet for many years. I would only speak about things that were safe and acceptable. Don't rock the boat. Yet, there was always something inside of me burning to get out.

Fear seems to be a major part of the human experience. This is why it is so important to learn to realize that there is something inside of us so powerful it actually created the very world we live in. You see, we create our own realities with our thoughts. Garbage in, equals garbage out. What we believe we receive. If you doubt, you go without. These are all catch phrases you may have heard many times before. There is a reason these phrases have been so popular, it's because there is great truth to them. The only thing that holds us back is ourselves. And we usually hold ourselves back with our thoughts of fear. Now, as I travel around the world teaching personal empowerment in its varied forms, I speak my truth. Even though all that I say may not be acceptable to everyone, the words I speak set my soul free. I have reclaimed my power—fear no longer controls my voice. Where is fear holding you back in life?

Exercise

Are you ready to reveal what's been holding you back? One of your most powerful tools on this journey of self-discovery and personal freedom is the pen and paper. So here we go:

1. Make a list all the things you want to do, be or have, but feel blocked in attaining them.
2. Now for each item listed, write down how not doing it, being it or having it has served to keep you safe. This is the very thing that is holding you back. If you are ready to move forward, continue with the next step.
3. For each item listed explore ways in which you can move forward and still feel safe. You are a creative being with lots of creative potential. You can figure this out, and once you figure it out, make a commitment to yourself to embrace your power and start moving your life forward, one day at a time. Develop an action plan, set some powerful goals. And by all means, start today. We are on Day 3 of this powerful journey to change your life. You have to participate fully!

Affirmation

Commit the following positive affirmation to memory, and silently recite it to yourself throughout the day whenever you think of it, or to counter any negative thoughts, or to simply reinforce the idea that anything is possible in an abundant universe.

Obstacles are merely open doors for my magnificence to shine through.

Visualization

As you close your eyes tonight, visualize a beautiful big bright sun above your body. Feel the sun shining its rays down upon you and know that these are golden rays of prosperity. Allow these rays of prosperity to completely cover your body. Feel yourself starting to breathe in these golden rays of prosperity. The light of prosperity fills your entire being, lighting you up, clearing away from your mind, conscious and subconscious, any limiting thoughts or belief systems that would prevent your having it all. Feel these golden warm rays of love mending and healing anything within your emotional memory that would limit your having it all. Feel your entire body, mind and emotions washed over, cleansed and healed by the ever prevailing waves of prosperity. Prosperity cannot co-exist with anything unlike it so just allow yourself to drift off to sleep knowing your body, mind, and spirit are being reprogrammed, all old belief systems reprogrammed, all negative emotions and self-sabotaging behaviors erased as the golden rays of prosperity fill your entire being. Sleep well.

Journal

You may use this space or your own journal to write down any thoughts, feelings, ideas or insights that may have come up for you during the exercise.

DAY 4
SELF-AWARENESS

What Moves Me Forward?

Commentary

Are you moved into action more quickly when you are pushed by pain, or pulled by pleasure? I love to eat. It brings me great pleasure. But it causes me pain when I overindulge. However, the pain of overeating never stopped me from overeating as I seem to be more pulled by pleasure. I use to smoke cigarettes because it made me feel good in the moment. Had I been motivated more by pain, I would never have overeaten because the results were always painful; and I would have quit smoking immediately after choking on the first cigarette. I believe we are all motivated by pain and by pleasure, the key is to know which motivates and moves you to action more quickly. Once you know this about yourself, you can use it to move you forward and begin to embrace your power more quickly.

If you are motivated more by pain, in order to embrace your power, you need to discover for yourself just how painful it will be at the end of your life when you have not lived your life to the fullest. That will help to motivate you to move forward towards your greatness. If you are motivated more by pleasure, you must see the joy you will have at the end of your life, knowing you are all used up, knowing you did it big and you did your very best. Whatever moves you forward, whether you must be pushed by pain or pulled more by pleasure, learn to work with it in a way that serves your embracing your power and leading a more fulfilling and rewarding life.

Exercise

Take time to go into quiet contemplation. Think of the last time you were motivated to get something done that you considered big. Now think of what made you decide to move on it. Was it that you were looking to get something wonderful, or was it that you were looking to move away from something not so wonderful.

Do this exercise with several things you consider big moves you've made in your life to get an idea as to whether you move more quickly toward pleasure or more quickly away from pain. Once you know your programming, start to figure out ways to use it to help you grow. If it takes pain to motivate you, think of all the bad things that could happen if you don't grow and do whatever it is you need to do. If it takes pleasure to motivate you, think of all the good things that could happen if you do grow and do whatever it is you must do. Neither way is better than the other; it's about knowing yourself and how you operate.

Affirmation

Commit the following positive affirmation to memory, and silently recite it to yourself throughout the day whenever you think of it, or to counter any negative thoughts, or to simply reinforce the idea that anything is possible in an abundant universe.

I enjoy the freedom of moving forward.

Visualization

Once again, as you drift off to sleep, visualize your best life possible—don't hold anything back. Picture your dream home, car, touch the fabrics of the fine clothing you wear, feel the excitement of the romance in your life, feel the closeness and love of your family and the quality of the deep friendships you've attracted into your life. See yourself giving joyously and generously to your favorite charity, smile as you write the large check. Visualize yourself doing the work you love to do and being richly rewarded and appreciated for it. Invite all of your senses to participate. See the surroundings, smell the air, taste the wine, touch the textures, hear the voices of appreciation. Enjoy your dreams as they soon become realities. Sleep well.

Journal

You may use this space or your own journal to write down any thoughts, feelings, ideas or insights that may have come up for you during the exercise.

Self-Acceptance
Steps 5 through 8

Honoring Who You Are

*Once you are clear about who you are
you then need to accept yourself fully and completely
in order to start embracing your power.*

DAY 5
SELF-ACCEPTANCE

Honoring My Own Opinions

Commentary

"You are wrong, and you clearly aren't thinking right." On several occasions I was told that I was not thinking properly and that there was something wrong with my thinking just because I didn't agree with what was being said. And, as a Wimpy Wanna, I would give in and agree just to keep the peace. I would disregard my own opinion for the sake of being accepted by another. I was a classic people-pleaser with a fear of being or even appearing to be wrong. I found myself disregarding the power of my own experience in favor of other people's thoughts, opinions and ideas. It just felt easier than thinking for myself and risking being wrong. Unfortunately that "ease" came with a price. I felt undervalued, underappreciated and eventually unheard because that's how I was treating myself. It was a long time before I even knew what *my* thoughts were.

Well, I have learned that I have a right to my opinion just like everyone else has a right to theirs. Just because our opinions may differ, does not make you right and me wrong or vice versa. One of the reasons I used to give in so easily was because I was always comparing my ability to think to that of my parents, both great thinkers. So, I would feel inadequate because I didn't think I could ever measure up to them. Then,

I began to be my own champion; valuing, appreciating. and welcoming my own opinions as relevant. My experience is the only one where I am a certified expert. Accepting my thoughts and honoring my own opinions put me on the road to fully accepting myself and embracing my power.

Exercise

Think back to a time when you were in a situation where you had a difference of opinion from someone you cared about. Recall how you really felt during that exchange. Did you feel weakened, hurt and/or angry? If thinking about it brings back those feelings, it means you are giving your power away to something that happened in the past. It means that you still have a negative emotional charge around it. In order to take back your power, you must discharge situations that leave a negative imprint upon you. So, let's neutralize it right now. See yourself in this situation once again, but this time, see the person before you as a cartoon character with big floppy ears and a long funny nose. And, as this person is saying these things to you, looking ever so silly, notice how hard it is for you to keep from laughing out loud. Keep playing this same scenario over and over in your mind, from the beginning of the conversation to the end, until you notice that you are no longer bothered by the words spoken when you think about it. You've taken back your power.

Affirmation

Commit the following positive affirmation to memory, and silently recite it to yourself throughout the day whenever you think of it, or to counter any negative thoughts, or to simply reinforce the idea that accepting all of who you are is easy.

My Mind Is the Mind of Infinite Intelligence.

Visualization

Review today's exercise just prior to sleep and focus on how you felt differently when you didn't take the situation so seriously. As the saying goes, "don't sweat the small stuff, and, it's all small stuff." If you are still bothered by the situation after running the story over and over in your mind, run it again a few times as you go to sleep, taking it deep into your subconscious. Visualize yourself speaking to this person who looks very silly and who is trying to disagree with you or put you down. Just see yourself laughing inside as you drift off to sleep. If you were successful in neutralizing the situation in your mind during the exercise today, you may want to take this opportunity to work on another similar situation. Take the time to neutralize any and all negative emotional charges from your past by seeing them differently and not taking them so seriously.

Journal

You may use this space or your own journal to write down any thoughts, feelings, ideas or insights that may have come up for you during the exercise.

DAY 6
SELF-ACCEPTANCE

Oh How I Adore Thee (Me)

Commentary

What? You want me to walk down an aisle, look into a mirror and profess my love for myself? This had to be one of the silliest things I had ever heard of. Ms. Wanda, my Life Coach had designed a sacred self-marriage ceremony for women and wanted me to participate. Although it sounded silly, I trusted her so I decided to give it a try. The major components of the program is to watch yourself walk down an aisle toward a full length mirror, come face-to-face with yourself, and then speak kind, loving, wonderful words to yourself as you look in the mirror. As I approached the mirror, at that moment, I realized how important it is to accept yourself fully and completely. I felt like I had taken back my power from what society thought about me. No matter what anyone else thinks, I am totally adorable and lovable.

As strange as it may seem, we often find it easier to highlight what we don't like about ourselves rather than acknowledge what we do like about ourselves. If you can't adore yourself, know that the door is not open for you to allow others to adore you. If others were to try, you might be in such denial you wouldn't believe them and unconsciously you may even find a way to get them out of your life! Let us no longer be shy. Let us as powerful beings learn to love and adore that which God has created. Let us not be boastful, but joyous in the glory that we are.

Exercise

Write out your definition of the word "adore." Now make a list of the things you adore about someone you love or like very much. Now make a list of the things you adore about yourself and why. Another word for adore could be "admire."

Example: I adore the way I handle people who panic over small things—because I can see the bigger picture which empowers me to have compassion and bring peace to the situation.

Affirmation

Commit the following positive affirmation to memory, and silently recite it to yourself throughout the day whenever you think of it, or to counter any negative thoughts, or to simply reinforce the idea that anything is possible in an abundant universe.

I adore the me that I have become.

Visualization

See yourself walking down an aisle lined with all of your family and friends, and at the end of the aisle is a full length mirror and a very large vase of your favorite flowers on each side and a very loving Spirit Guide standing next to the mirror waiting for you as you walk ever so slowly down the aisle, contemplating each step towards total self-acceptance. As you approach the mirror you notice how you seem to be outside of your body, observing yourself walking. You notice how you adore that person walking toward the mirror. You admire their willingness to love him/herself to accept him/herself. And as this person (you) approaches the mirror you start reciting words of grace, beauty and admiration for yourself. You start to fill up with love and appreciation knowing all that you've been through in your life, all that you have survived, all that you have given, all that you have held on to, all that you have been forced to let go of. You see before you a powerful person that you so love, adore and admire. You adore the person you have become.

Journal

You may use this space or your own journal to write down any thoughts, feelings, ideas or insights that may have come up for you during the exercise.

DAY 7
SELF-ACCEPTANCE

Free Your Mind and Your Body Will Follow

Commentary

How could this be! My bathroom scales had betrayed me! I had been so good! I had done all the right things, followed my diet religiously, been a really good girl. Well, instead of the scale going down, it actually went up! I was so completely devastated I didn't know what to do. My entire day was ruined. I really needed my Life Coach. I dragged through the day, my session wasn't until that evening. Finally the time came when I could share. I spoke about how the scale had ruined my day. The session revealed the truth. I had given my power away to the scale. I allowed the number on my bathroom scale to dictate how I would feel the entire day. I felt like a failure, weak, and utterly defeated. I had to realize that I was more than a number on a scale, and I had to learn to accept myself regardless of appearance. Once I got it, I took back my power. I refused to allow my emotions to be controlled by the scale. In fact I decided I would not get back on it for a while. I had to decide, make up my mind, that it didn't matter what was on the scale, I was going to be okay. It was a few weeks before I climbed back on that scale, only to find that I had lost weight. I only needed to free my mind so my body could follow.

Exercise

Pick something that could ruin your day. It could be anything from the number on the bathroom scale, missing a flight or losing that important deal, to losing someone you love. Now image this thing happening to you and see what your normal reaction would be. Now imagine yourself 10 years older, 20 years older, 30 years or maybe even 50 years older and a lot wiser. See how you would now handle the same situation as a more mature person. Now decide to be that more mature person today, right here and right now. Just be it. Release your drama and step into your wisdom. Embrace your power.

Affirmation

Commit the following positive affirmation to memory, and silently recite it to yourself throughout the day whenever you think of it, or to counter any negative thoughts, or to simply reinforce the idea that anything is possible in an abundant universe.

My body reflects the beauty of my inner thoughts.

Visualization

See yourself standing before a full length mirror, and before you is the image of the perfect body: lean, healthy, fine, fit and full of energy and vitality. Realize that this is the blueprint of perfection within you. Now, as you visualize this perfect body in the mirror allow the image to start to shift to what you normally see when you look in the mirror. As the image starts to shift to what you would consider the not-so-perfect body, allow your mind to say, "This *is my* perfect body today. I look exactly how I am supposed to look right now and for whatever reason. And, I am beautiful." Feel your mind beginning to release all the judgments you have been holding onto about the way you look. See the mirror glowing as you radiate your inner beauty into it. Feel good about acknowledging your wonderful body just the way it is, honoring it, and loving all of who you are as you drift off to sleep. Sleep well.

Journal

You may use this space or your own journal to write down any thoughts, feelings, ideas or insights that may have come up for you during the exercise.

DAY 8
SELF-ACCEPTANCE

How Can I Start Loving Myself More?

Commentary

Walking down the aisle in the sacred self-marriage cere-mony, professing my love for myself was only the beginning. I had to honor those new vows I had laid out for myself and start living my life in a way that supported my loving and accepting myself more. I use to think smoking cigarettes was loving myself. It sounds ridiculous but it made sense to me at the time. When I smoked a cigarette, I felt good. Smoking calmed my nerves and allowed a break from a hectic sched-ule. It also kept me company when I felt alone. When I decided to quit, one of the things I looked at was the essence of the good feelings I got from smoking. I realized that the same soothing, calming break I got when I inhaled cigarette smoke, I felt just from taking a deep cleansing breath of air. It took more focus and effort to sit still and take a deep breath, but it worked, and the long term effects of taking deep breaths are much better than the long term consequences of smoking. Now that I've quit smoking, I recognize that one of the most important aspects of self-love is self-care. I've learned that you take care of things you love and that must include you.

Exercise

Again, with pen and paper before you, allow yourself to relax by taking a couple of deep breaths. Once you are centered, ask yourself the following questions, writing down your responses:

1. Where am I not loving myself enough (where are you unhappy)?
2. What can I do to change this situation?
3. Am I able to make the necessary changes right now? If not, when can I begin?
4. Am I willing to start loving myself more despite the circumstances?

Once you are clear about what needs to be done, incorporate these things into the action plan you started on Day 3 for changing your life.

Affirmation

Commit the following positive affirmation to memory, and silently recite it to yourself throughout the day whenever you think of it, or to counter any negative thoughts, or to simply reinforce the idea that anything is possible in an abundant universe.

I have Supreme Love for all that I Am.

Visualization

See yourself as a small child. And, also see yourself as an adult gazing into the eyes of that small child. Look into those beautiful, innocent eyes with love and compassion. Sense that this child needs only one thing from you, and that is your love. Feel the love stirring in the center of your heart. Feel this warm vibration as energy begins to radiate out from you towards this child in front of you. See a beam of beautiful light particles dancing from the center of your heart to the center of this child's heart. Allow your imagination to take you deeper, to feel the love between the two of you like you've never felt love before.

Now see yourself gently take this child into your arms, lovingly embracing this child, telling him/her that you love him/her and that you will always be there. No matter what, you will always love them first. Feel the warm embrace shifting into a merging of the two of you so that the essence of the child becomes one with you. Feel the child within you feeling cared for and nurtured and feeling safe. Know that as you protect this child, you are protecting and loving yourself. This is your first responsibility, to take care of and love yourself first. Never allow anyone to misuse you or abuse you because you are caring for someone quite precious, your inner child.

Journal

You may use this space or your own journal to write down any thoughts, feelings, ideas or insights that may have come up for you during the exercise.

Self-Love
Steps 9 through 12

Learning Self-Care

Once you have learned to accept yourself
more fully, you will then want to begin
taking better care of yourself,
this is called self-love.

DAY 9
SELF-LOVE

Forgiving And Releasing The Past

Commentary

To forgive is not always easy. My grandfather was a shining example to me of the power of forgiveness. It started when his son, my father, Dr. Martin Luther King, Jr., was killed. He had to live with that without carrying any bitterness or hatred in his heart. And then, six years later, he would have to experience loss all over again. This time his wife, whom we called Big Mama, his helpmate of more than 47 years was gunned down while she was playing the organ during a Sunday morning church service. My grandfather, in all of his pain, went to the jailhouse that very same evening and said to the gunman, "Son I don't understand you, but I forgive you." His Christian walk kept him strong. Now when I am faced with situations that seem unforgivable, I see my grandfather's face and hear him say, "Hate is too great a burden to bear."

Exercise

Get yourself some 3" x 5" index cards, or use small pieces of paper. On each card or piece of paper, write down the name of a person in your past that you would like to forgive.

Find a comfortable siting position, take a few deep breaths and relax holding the cards in your hand. Imagine yourself filled with love, light and compassion for the world. Breathe it in.

Ask God for the strength and the courage that it takes to forgive.

One card at a time:

1. Hold up a card so you can see the name on it.
2. While looking at the name, image that person sitting before you now.
3. Say to that person out loud, "I forgive you for _____."
4. Now, silently bless them by saying a prayer for their well-being.

True forgiveness is when you can wish the other person well. When you can do this, you are releasing any grudges and taking back your power. To hold a grudge against someone is like you taking poison and expecting the other person to die. Bless the mess and move on. Do this exercise with each index card you have written a name on. You can do this over a period of several days if that's more comfortable, but make sure you fully connect with your feelings on a soul level.

Affirmation

Commit the following positive affirmation to memory, and silently recite it to yourself throughout the day whenever you think of it, or to counter any negative thoughts, or to simply reinforce the idea that God is right where you are and its okay to let go and forgive.

I release the past freeing
myself and everyone else.

Visualization

Imagine each person you want to forgive standing in a line before you. As the first person steps up to greet you, look into their eyes and say to them, "I am now free and so are you." See the two of you bow your heads in honor of each other and then watch that person turn and walk away. Then see the next person in line step up to greet you. Grant that person the same freedom and dismiss them. Do this for each person you need to release and at the end of the line your work is done. Sleep well.

Journal

You may use this space or your own journal to write down any thoughts, feelings, ideas or insights that may have come up for you during the exercise.

DAY 10
SELF-LOVE

Being Kinder to Myself

Commentary

Was it just me, or do most people spend a lot of time beating up on themselves? What does it mean to be kind to one's self? For me, it means to stop beating up on yourself when you do something wrong or make a stupid mistake. It means taking a break when you need one and not working yourself to death. It means taking good care of your body, feeding your mind with positive thoughts, uplifting your spirit by being of good cheer, and taking care of yourself by having healthy boundaries. It means loving yourself enough to know when you must put your needs first.

To embrace your power, you must learn to be kind to yourself. If you become more powerful and have not learned kindness and self-care, you will only beat up on yourself with more force and conviction when things go wrong. Not good. So it is imperative that you start today being kinder to yourself so that as you embrace your power, you become a better person, not only for you, but for those around you as well.

Exercise

The first step in being kinder to yourself is to become aware of when you are not being so kind. So take one day and carry with you your magnificent pen and paper. Jot down each time you notice that you've said something to yourself or to someone else that was not so kind about yourself. You might note such statements as, "I'm so fat," or "I can never do anything right," etc. Self-talk is a dead give-away about how you are unconsciously treating yourself. Also jot down when you physically bump or bruise yourself, or drop something. Note your thoughts in that moment.

Once you have become more aware of the things you are saying, you can make a conscious effort to stop the negative chatter and replace it with something more positive, or nothing at all.

Affirmation

Commit the following positive affirmation to memory, and silently recite it to yourself throughout the day whenever you think of it, or to counter any negative thoughts, or to simply reinforce the idea that anything is possible in an abundant universe.

I am in love with the me that I am becoming.

Visualization

Imagine how your life would be different if you were kinder to yourself. How would you treat yourself differently? How different would your self-talk be? How different would your world look through your eyes? How would people see you differently? How would you show up differently in the world. Take back your power through kindness, and imagine what a better world you will be creating for yourself. Imagine it, see it, feel it, believe in it and sleep well.

Journal

You may use this space or your own journal to write down any thoughts, feelings, ideas or insights that may have come up for you during the exercise.

DAY 11
SELF-LOVE

Setting Clear Boundaries for Others

Commentary

I was raised in a family that emphasized the importance of loving and supporting each other. Yes, there were spats between us siblings from time to time, but for the most part we stuck together like glue. And then the day came. I had to make a very important decision that looked like I wasn't supporting one of my siblings. I had to say "no" which was not easy for me, especially within this very loving and supportive family. But, there was no other answer for me other than "no" and this forced me to embrace my power, stand in my truth, and stand up for what I knew was right for my soul. There is no way I could have come to this decision if I did not have clear personal boundaries already in place. I had to have enough self-love that I would not allow anyone to cross those boundaries, not even a loved one.

Sometimes, in order to honor your boundaries you just have to practice tough love. Saying "no" can be the toughest thing you'll ever have to say to someone you love. Self-love is about treating yourself with respect and having very clear boundaries so that others learn to respect you as well.

Exercise

You can discover where you have boundary issues by looking at all the places in your life where you are doing things you don't like doing, including working in a job that you don't like. It may be difficult to quit a job you don't like, but it would make it easier to find the little things about the job that you do like and start focusing on those.

If you have a hard time saying "no," practice looking down and pausing before answering someone's request. When you look downward, you are accessing your feelings. Pause to get a sense of how saying "yes" would make you feel. It if doesn't feel good, you must learn to say "no." If you can't say "no," tell them that you need time to "think about it" and walk away. It can be easier to find clarity when you are alone.

Decide on all those things you are doing that you don't like, and start to incorporate into your plan of action steps that will remove you from doing those things in the future. Start working on this one day at a time.

Affirmation

Commit the following positive affirmation to memory, and silently recite it to yourself throughout the day whenever you think of it, or to counter any negative thoughts, or to simply reinforce the idea that anything is possible in an abundant universe.

My boundaries are clear,
honored, and respected by all.

Visualization

See yourself surrounded by difficult people, people who want something from you, people who dishonor or disrespect you, people who push your buttons.

Now visualize a beautiful beam of white light coming down from the heavens surrounding you in a bubble of love, creating a boundary between you and them, acting as a filter. Only God-like qualities are allowed to penetrate this beautiful bubble of light, qualities such as love, honor, respect, peace, joy, grace, appreciation, admiration, celebration. Know that there is a silent understanding now between you and all these people. They realize they can no longer push your buttons. They can no longer dishonor you for you are within the light, you are protected, all is well in your world.

See yourself living in this beautiful light at all times. Walking in the light of pure love and respect. Be free now. Embrace your power and sleep well.

Journal

You may use this space or your own journal to write down any thoughts, feelings, ideas or insights that may have come up for you during the exercise.

DAY 12

SELF-LOVE

A Schedule That Supports My Personal Needs

Commentary

Late night soaps drained my energy. Every night I would give my power away to the world of soap operas. I would record them during the day and then stay up watching them far into the night. This was my way of winding down and escaping from my busy days. However, it had its price as mornings were often tough due to a lack of sleep. I had to look at why I needed to escape from the day. It was because I didn't have a schedule that supported my personal needs. My schedule was based on what everyone else needed from me.

Before I knew God was my source, and I thought I was my source, I worked all the time. I had no play time. If I did, it often consisted of things I could do that were unhealthy or mischievous, just to balance out all the hard work. This was how I would subconsciously reward myself for working so hard. Now I know that no matter how hard I work, I am sustained by something beyond me and beyond my personal ability to "make" things happen. So I learned to surrender, to be guided, to be still enough to listen. Now I find that when I take time for play, the type of play I'm drawn to is more healing, more nurturing to my soul, more satisfying overall. And, there are no repercussions, no hangovers, no headaches.

Exercise

Are you taking enough time for yourself? Look over your last month-at-a-glance calendar. If you don't use a month-at-a-glance, create one for this exercise. Create one for the last two months. Now get two highlighters, one pink and one green. Highlight on your calendar in pink all the things you did that drained your energy, things you did because you had to but didn't really want to. Now highlight in green all the things you did that were nurturing, healing, fun, and gave you energy. Now review your calendar for the past couple of months and see if there is more green or pink. Then you can decide if you need to have more time for you. If so, add more fun things to your action plan. Plan a vacation or some other activities that bring you healthy healing joy.

Affirmation

Commit the following positive affirmation to memory, and silently recite it to yourself throughout the day whenever you think of it, or to counter any negative thoughts, or to simply reinforce the idea that anything is possible in an abundant universe.

Playing creates more prosperity
by freeing up my creative energy.

Visualization

See yourself in your ideal vacation setting, maybe it's on a luxury cruise, hiking in the wilderness, visiting far away cultures. Whatever your dream vacation may be, see yourself in that setting now. Notice how easy it is to take yourself there in your mind. Know that everything IS a state of mind. Relax into this peaceful and/or exciting setting and start to enjoy your life. Know that you can feel this kind of peace and/or excitement anytime you want or need to just by visiting this special place in your mind.

Invite all of your senses to participate. See all of the elements of your vacation, taste the foods, feel the textures around you, smell the aromas in the air, listen to the sounds around you. Fully embrace this place and take it into dream state with you. Sleep well.

Journal

You may use this space or your own journal to write down any thoughts, feelings, ideas or insights that may have come up for you during the exercise.

Self-Discipline
Steps 13 through 16

Willingness to Grow

Willingness moves mountains.
Where there is a will, there is a way.

DAY 13
SELF-DISCIPLINE

What Needs to Be Removed from My Life?

Commentary

Let's see... there was John, and Tim, and Rachel who took more than they gave. Then there was Mark who I had a hard time getting over; he really broke my heart. Oh yes, let's not forget the broken promises, the hurts, and the slights. All this old baggage I carried around needed to be removed from my life. You see, when you harbor baggage it takes up space within you, space that should be used for embracing your power. You have to come clean in order to have all the power you desire to create the life you desire. You can't think that new stuff will come when you continue to hold on to old stuff. It doesn't work that way. I really had a hard time releasing people, even if I knew they were toxic for my life. I also had to release unresolved emotions, limiting beliefs and old behavior patterns that no longer served me. Much had to be released from my life in order for me to embrace my power. And, I must say, letting go is always a step-by-step process.

Exercise

As we grow up there are certain instances that make emotional imprints upon us. It doesn't matter if they are good or bad things, just that they are somehow significant to us. Close your eyes and start to recall each significant incident in your life from as far back as you can remember all the way up to present time. Make a brief recording of each, the good and the bad, in your journal.

And now looking over those significant incidents, decide which ones no longer serve you and need to be removed from your life. Highlight or checkmark those incidents.

Now for each incident that needs to be removed. See the incident the way you remember it and notice how you feel about it. Then run the scene backwards in your mind as though you are erasing it. Run it backwards over and over again, from the beginning of the memory to the end, until you notice that you start to feel differently about it, until it has become neutralized. Reversing an incident will not delete it from your memory, it will simply help to remove any emotional charge associated with it so that the incident is no longer running your life. You get to embrace more of your power by being more in charge of your emotions.

Affirmation

Commit the following positive affirmation to memory, and silently recite it to yourself throughout the day whenever you think of it, or to counter any negative thoughts, or to simply reinforce the idea that anything is possible in an abundant universe.

*I release the past and fully embrace
all of my power now.*

Visualization

Once again, as you drift off to sleep visualize your best life. See yourself accomplishing something you've been working towards for a long time. See everyone around you complimenting you on a job well done. Feel the feeling of success deep down in your bones. Breath in victory and total satisfaction. Fall in love with yourself tonight as you drift off to sleep. Totally feel the power of who you are. Sleep well.

Journal

You may use this space or your own journal to write down any thoughts, feelings, ideas or insights that may have come up for you during the exercise.

DAY 14
SELF-DISCIPLINE

What Needs to Be Added to My Life?

Commentary

Swinging through the trees without a solid place to land. That was my life when I was younger. I was busy doing for everyone else and not disciplined enough to take care of myself. I had religion, but I needed a deeper connection with God.I knew about God, but I was too busy seeking to please others and not taking the time to develop a deeper relationship and really get to know God.

The spiritual teacher, Ram Das, talks about a lady that was sitting in his audience as he was speaking about finding God. During the break, he asked this woman what she did to find God. She said she crocheted. I love this because it lets you know there is no right or wrong way to find God. I believe that we are all looking for one thing and that is love, the love that brings about peace of mind. And I also believe that the peace we seek comes from the core of our beings, not from anything outside of us. What I needed to add to my life was a deeper connection to the God within me. God shows up in many ways for different people. For some it may be meditation. For others it may be a walk on the beach, sitting in church, or crocheting.

For me it was stillness. I had to learn to be still to find my guidance which ultimately led to more peace of mind. What do you need in order to find more peace, more love, more joy? Is your life filled with that already, or does more of it need to be added to your life?

Exercise

In your handy, dandy journal of change and transformation, make a list of the things that make you feel good inside; those things that make you feel more connected. Now scan your life and notice how many of those things are missing from your life.

Look back over your calendar, organizer, palm pilot, etc., for the last 30 days. Review your highlighted calendar from the exercise for Day 12. Count the number of days you did things that really made you feel good inside, connected. If you find that you didn't do at least one thing each day to make you feel connected, you are giving your power away to external circumstances, and it's time to add more things into your life that help you to feel good about yourself and to feel connected. The only way to embrace your power is to feel good about yourself through the daily practice of that which makes you feel connected, and through having the discipline to maintain that practice.

Affirmation

Commit the following positive affirmation to memory, and silently recite it to yourself throughout the day whenever you think of it, or to counter any negative thoughts, or to simply reinforce the idea that anything is possible in an abundant universe.

All that I need is added unto me now.

Visualization

Tonight, see yourself doing the thing or things that bring you the greatest joy, peace, and sense of well-being. See yourself doing them fully without restriction or limitation. See yourself free.

Journal

You may use this space or your own journal to write down any thoughts, feelings, ideas or insights that may have come up for you during the exercise.

DAY 15

SELF-DISCIPLINE

Declaring What is Sacred in My Life

Commentary

Doctor's diagnosis, atrial fibrillation (irregular heart beat). My mouth dropped. Why me. What does this mean? The word "sacred" means precious. We take so much for granted, like the air we breathe, the very feet that carry us. My heart beat became so much more precious to me when the doctor said it was not regular and I might need surgery to correct it. How often do you think about your heart? About your life? Do you consider yourself a precious being? You can't fully embrace your power until you realize that the very breath you are breathing is sacred.

Since I found out how sacred my heart is, I started asking myself about other things in my life that I consider sacred. When you do this life inventory, you start wondering why you have so much stuff in your life that is just dead weight holding you back, taking up your time and energy. I learned to let go of things that were not sacred to me so that my life could be filled with more things that I hold dear and precious. What have you declared sacred in your life? Are those things really good and healthy for you? Check it out—honestly.

Exercise

Ask yourself the following questions :

- What/who are you taking for granted?
- What do you feel is precious about that person or thing?
- How can you demonstrate that s/he or it is precious to you?
- Will you do it?
- When?
- What/who have you declared sacred in your life that is really toxic for you?
- What will you do to remove them from your life?
- Will you do it?
- When?

Add these things to your Action Plan.

Affirmation

Commit the following positive affirmation to memory, and silently recite it to yourself throughout the day whenever you think of it, or to counter any negative thoughts, or to simply reinforce the idea that anything is possible in an abundant universe.

My life is sacred and precious
as I am a child of the Most High.

Visualization

Whatever you have declared in your life to be the most sacred, see yourself embracing it. If it is intangible, allow it to present itself to you in the shape of a sacred symbol so that you might embrace the symbol. See yourself holding that which is sacred and feel the energy of it pour through your entire being. Fill yourself up with that which is sacred to you. Feel your body beginning to pulsate and vibrate to a sacred melody. Allow this inner rhythm to carry you away, into a deep and relaxing sleep.

Journal

You may use this space or your own journal to write down any thoughts, feelings, ideas or insights that may have come up for you during the exercise.

DAY 16
SELF-DISCIPLINE

Learning to Be Still

Commentary

My life came to a stop, a complete standstill for about a day when I was diagnosed with a mild heart condition. My world was so crazy busy that not only were my thoughts always racing ahead, but my heartbeat started racing as well. I became short of breath with anxiety, and panic attacks would visit me frequently. My spirit said I needed to be still. Thankfully, I have learned that what many people perceive as problems are cleverly disguised opportunities for growth. This so-called heart condition stopped me from working out like a maniac, stopped me from working myself into an early grave. When you are too busy to meditate, something is bound to slow you down. A friend introduced me to TM, Transcendental Meditation. I invested in private training immediately and began a practice of stillness. It took self-discipline to keep it up, but I knew I needed to do this for my health, for my peace of mind. You have to decide for yourself just how important it is for you to slow down, to take the time to just be still. It is in the stillness that healing takes place. It is in the silence that you hear your truth. And it is in peaceful contemplation and meditation that all you are searching for is revealed.

Exercise

You may want to try TM or some other formal meditation practice, but here is an exercise you can get started with right away. Start by sitting at the same time each day for about 10-15 minutes and just focusing on your breath. Take a full breath in and fill your belly with air. Hold it for a few seconds, then release. Do this about ten times. Then just sit and feel the energy of relaxation moving through your body as you breathe normally. As you start to appreciate this sensation you will want to be still longer and more often, and soon you will find yourself open to receive guidance from the still small voice within. There are other stillness exercises, such as using a mantra, focusing on a candle flame or simply watching your breath. Don't become confused by all the different meditation practices out there, just sit in the stillness, and the right practice will soon find you.

Affirmation

Commit the following positive affirmation to memory, and silently recite it to yourself throughout the day whenever you think of it, or to counter any negative thoughts, or to simply reinforce the idea that anything is possible in an abundant universe.

Within the stillness, I am whole.

Visualization

See yourself sitting on a mountain top, or any wonderful place that makes you feel your power and the power of the Universe. Imagine yourself sitting on the ground cross legged. You have drawn a large circle around you, and you are in the center of this circle. The circle is your doorway to the outer world. Within this circle is your inner world. You have decided to sit within your inner world for 40 days and nights, and you shall not be moved until the point of enlightenment.

You notice that you start to hear songs and spiritual chants being sung in your head; you hear the songs of birds as nature bows down in celebration of your stillness. You see flowers blooming on the parameters of the circle awaiting your rising. You see yourself in deep meditation knowing, enjoying and appreciating the power of stillness as you drift off into pure bliss, into a deep peaceful sleep.

Journal

You may use this space or your own journal to write down any thoughts, feelings, ideas or insights that may have come up for you during the exercise.

Self-Confidence
Steps 17 through 20

Knowing You Are Enough

DAY 17
SELF-CONFIDENCE

Building Upon Feelings of Success

Commentary

There I was, standing before hundreds of people, 5 minutes into a show and my voice completely left me. My greatest fear found me. I could not continue and had to leave the stage. My dear friend and stage manager prayed over me and someone got me some throat spray. The audience waited patiently for more than 30 minutes while I was being taken care of backstage. Once I was able to pull myself together and go back on stage, the crowd applauded and I started over. Because I had very little voice, I could not simply rely on my voice. I had to go deeper into the characters and find the essence of what they were saying in the moment. It needed to be conveyed not only through what little voice I had left, but through my body, and through my intention. I approached the whole experience from a deeper place than ever before. I had to surrender and trust. Guess what? I did an incredible job. After receiving a very long standing ovation at the conclusion of the show, my director commented that I should lose my voice for every performance. This experience created a feeling of success for me. I no longer carried the fear that if I lost my voice, life would be over. I previously thought I would be so embarrassed, so ashamed, I would never recover from it. It actually ended up being a blessing and a wonderful breakthrough in my career. What I feared became one of my greater moments of success. I now can use this experience and these feelings of success to transform fear or doubt about anything in my life into something positive. This is indeed a place of empowerment.

Exercise

Think of a so-called failure of your own. Now think of a success you've had. Now, holding both yours hands face up out in front of you, place the energy of the failure in one hand and the energy of the success in your other hand. Now pour the energy from the hand filled with success into the hand where there is the failure energy and know that the energy of failure is being transformed into success because that is all it really is anyway. It is only your perception that has labeled it something different.

Affirmation

Commit the following positive affirmation to memory, and silently recite it to yourself throughout the day whenever you think of it, or to counter any negative thoughts, or to simply reinforce the idea that anything is possible in an abundant universe.

The success I create is my faith in action.

Visualization

Visualize yourself pouring love over any and all of your so-called failures or mistakes in life and transforming them into lessons learned and blessings gained. See them transforming into a pot of gold with a beautiful rainbow that travels from the pot of gold into the core of your being.

Journal

You may use this space or your own journal to write down any thoughts, feelings, ideas or insights that may have come up for you during the exercise.

DAY 18
SELF-CONFIDENCE

Countering Fear, Doubt, & Worry (Where is Your Focus?)

Commentary

I use to spend a lot of time thinking about what could go wrong, and needless to say, more often than not something would go wrong. You know what they say. "Whether you think you can, or think you can't, you are right." When I changed the ways in which I viewed things, things began to change. You can see all sides of the coin, but you must allow 90% of your focus to be on what you do want, not worrying about what you don't want. You can consider what could go wrong, but you don't have to live there in that state of mind. A pastor friend of mine, Rev. Dr. Michael Beckwith, says, "What you appreciate, appreciates." So it is imperative to keep my focus on those things that will bring love, joy, and peace into my life.

Exercise

Where is your focus throughout the day—take note. Stop and say to yourself, "Where is my attention right now? Is it on peace, or is it on something other than peace?" If your attention is not on peace, be gentle, have compassion for yourself and bring your focus back to peace. Pause throughout your day to check in with yourself. Ask, "Where is my focus in this present moment?"

Affirmation

Commit the following positive affirmation to memory, and silently recite it to yourself throughout the day whenever you think of it, or to counter any negative thoughts, or to simply reinforce the idea that anything is possible in an abundant universe.

My positive focus redefines my state of being.

Visualization

Little children like to spin in circles. Sufi dancers spin in beautiful circles. The Universe itself is circular. Circles are very powerful as they generate a build-up of energy. See yourself spinning in your mind's eye. Spinning around and around with your arms stretched outward, palms facing upward. Spinning around and around. Feel any negative energy thrown off you as you spin. Feel a vortex of energy beginning to build from your feet up. As the energy builds around your feet, moving up your torso and into your arms, neck and head, feel yourself becoming lighter and lighter. Let the energy carry you away, removing you from the realm of fear, doubt or any worries whatsoever. Spin like a child at play, spin like a sufi prayer dancer, spin like the lilies in the field that toil not. Spin into higher realms of consciousness as you drift off to sleep.

Journal

You may use this space or your own journal to write down any thoughts, feelings, ideas or insights that may have come up for you during the exercise.

DAY 19
SELF-CONFIDENCE

Standing Tall

Commentary

First position, stand up straight. I can still hear my mother's words. One of the gifts my mother gave me as a young child was to train me to walk with my head held high, with pride and dignity. Mother enrolled me in ballet classes, which greatly improved my posture and poise. Being a member of the King family was often like living in a fish bowl with everyone watching every move you made. So as children, we were taught to always be on our best behavior, to stand up tall and to look our best. Because of the way I carry myself, when people first meet me, they often say I walk like I'm royalty. Once they find out who I am, many continue to think of me as royalty. Well, I think we are all royalty, strong and proud beings blessed by God. So I stand tall and move from this place of confidence. When you show up confident in the world, the world responds accordingly, regardless of who you are or where you've come from. If you show up in the world as a Wimpy Wanna, the world has no choice but to treat you accordingly.

Exercise

Practice standing before a full length mirror. Stand tall and notice your feelings. Slump over and watch what happens to your feelings. In neuro-linguistic programming, we teach that if you are depressed, it is very difficult to remain depressed if you change your physiology. When you are looking down you are accessing your feelings. When a person is looking up they are either remembering something or dreaming up something new. They are accessing their mental thoughts rather than their feelings. Think the thoughts that make you feel good, stand tall and hold your head up with confidence.

Now practice walking as though there was a string pulling your head up. Walk with pride and dignity toward the mirror. Go ahead, practice. No one is watching—yet.

Affirmation

Commit the following positive affirmation to memory, and silently recite it to yourself throughout the day whenever you think of it, or to counter any negative thoughts, or to simply reinforce the idea that anything is possible in an abundant universe.

I stand tall and secure in who I am.

Visualization

They say most people have the fear of speaking before large crowds. But not you, not tonight. See yourself standing tall before a very large group of people. Feel your power. They are there to see you. You are the star of the show. Embrace your power, acknowledge you are worthy, they know it and you know it. It is not important the words you will speak at this moment, it is only important that you feel comfortable in your body. Even though everyone may be watching you, you feel comfortable. You see that you are standing tall and carrying yourself with grace, with ease and with total confidence in who you are.

Drift off to sleep watching yourself standing there before the large group of people and feeling good about yourself, totally standing in, and embracing your power.

Journal

You may use this space or your own journal to write down any thoughts, feelings, ideas or insights that may have come up for you during the exercise.

DAY 20

SELF-CONFIDENCE

Building Faith

Commentary

Packing up everything, leaving a big comfortable house in Atlanta behind, and moving into a small one-bedroom apartment in Los Angeles. Letting go of the good to make room for something better. That's called faith. My faith was strong, so it wasn't long before I began pursuing my dreams and was able to move out of the small apartment and into my own home again in a city that nurtured both my personal and professional growth. I took a leap of faith and followed my heart to Los Angeles. Having faith doesn't always mean things will turn out your way. Faith means you believe things always turn out the *best* way. Trying to do it our way requires major effort and mistakes or *mis-takes*. Surrendering to faith requires trust and opens the door to grace.

When my father was taken, I had to have faith that his life was not lived in vain, that he died for a good cause, that my family and I would survive and be okay. I had to walk in faith, to surrender my judgments to have peace and live for a brighter day.

There is an absolute supreme power in the universe governing all order. We demonstrate our faith in it each time we drive down the road, trusting the other drivers will stay on their side of the yellow line. We trust the sun is shining whether we see it or not. Many times we have hope for good to come out of things beyond our control. That which is beyond hope is faith, a knowingness that all is well and that God is in charge.

Exercise

Decide to do something today you've been afraid to do and have faith that it will all be okay.

Where do you need to surrender in your life—where are you holding on too tightly and not willing to live life fully? Where do you need to let God be in charge?

Now put yourself in the shoes of a very wise role model or consultant, teacher or guide and think of what that person would say to help you overcome any fears or obstacles. Make a list of all the things a role model would say to you. Don't judge anything that comes to mind, just write it down as though someone was dictating to you and you were simply taking notes.

Once you feel complete and the writing brings itself to a stop, look over your notes and decide which items feel right for you to do in order to overcome any fears or obstacles. Put a checkmark next to those items and then add to the list any other thoughts that may come to mind.

Finally, from the list of checked and added items, add to your plan of action as to what steps you will take to move forward, overcoming any obstacles and building your faith.

Affirmation

Commit the following positive affirmation to memory, and silently recite it to yourself throughout the day whenever you think of it, or to counter any negative thoughts, or to simply reinforce the idea that anything is possible in an abundant universe.

My faith expands day by day.

Visualization

See yourself wrapped in the arms of a Divine Mother, larger than life. Feel yourself being rocked gently to sleep hearing the soft sacred chants of the Supreme Mother Being singing: "I will hold you always, I will carry you, sleep my child in peace, you are safe, be free."

Journal

You may use this space or your own journal to write down any thoughts, feelings, ideas or insights that may have come up for you during the exercise.

Self-Expression
Steps 21 through 24

Expressing Your Magnificence

*Self-expression becomes a lot easier once you are clear
about who you are and what you want in life (your mission).
Self-expression happens more gracefully
when you can accept yourself,
when you have learned to love yourself
and are feeling confident in your skin.
Greater self-expression comes from being totally authentic.*

DAY 21
SELF-EXPRESSION

Speaking My Truth

Commentary

"Shut up!" He shouted at me as we walked down the street. I was so embarrassed at his sudden outbursts of anger. People stopped to watch for any response from me. I had none. I was so young, in school and this was a close friend that would just go off on me from time to time. He would scream and rant and rave at me about something I said or did that upset him and I would allow this public spectacle. Why? Because I was intimidated and paralyzed with fear. This behavior continued as other people came into my life, people who were dear to me and yet they sometimes said cruel and mean things to me. And, in an effort to keep the peace, I tolerated it! I was going along to get along. I would stand there and just take it, not saying a word.

One day I realized that my energy was being drained and my spirit was being diminished by tolerating negative behaviors because I wanted to keep the peace. The truth was I wasn't keeping the peace at all but merely covering up the dis-harmony, the dis-ease that characterized some of my relationships. I was not honoring myself enough to sincerely speak my truth in such a way that it could be heard and taken to heart. By allowing people to hurt me, I was not honoring these relationships that I insisted meant so much to me. The truth was, I was afraid. I was afraid of hurting their feelings or making them so angry we would no longer have a relationship; so I hinted at it, I joked around it. I did everything but speak directly to it. You see, when you speak directly to an issue, you must be ready and willing to experience the change that will result. Finally, the pain of remaining silent became too heavy a burden to bear and I had to summon the courage to speak my truth. Whether it's simply walking away from a hostile conversation or addressing an unkind remark, it is imperative to find that necessary courage.

Exercise

Make a list of all the people and things in your life you have been tolerating, things as small as a squeaky door to a broken relationship. Make your list. Then you have two choices: either make some changes or start accepting what is. It becomes something you no longer tolerate, it becomes something you accept, or something you are willing to have change. So next to each item on your list, write the word "accept" or "change." Now those things which you decide to accept, you must pray for peace until they no longer bother you. Those things you have the ability and desire to change, you must pray for guidance so that all is done with love and grace. Do the work, for it is only when you have peace of mind with those around you and your environment that you are able to fully embrace your power and find personal freedom.

Affirmation

Commit the following positive affirmation to memory, and silently recite it to yourself throughout the day whenever you think of it, or to counter any negative thoughts, or to simply reinforce the idea that anything is possible in an abundant universe.

My truth is spoken with love and integrity.

Visualization

See yourself entering a confrontation with someone you may find slightly intimidating. Remember to stand tall, never sit, stand so that energy is freely moving. Some people say they think better on their feet—it's because energy flows better when you are free to move around. So see yourself facing this person. Before you speak one word, feel yourself drop down into your center, bring your energy/focus to your solar plexus area. Get grounded and centered. Take a deep breath in and release it slowly, relaxing your entire body. Recite your affirmation silently to yourself: "My truth is spoken with love and integrity." Now see yourself beginning to speak. You may not hear the words spoken, but you are very aware of how you are feeling: strong, confident and no longer intimidated by this person before you. See this person responding to your words with gentleness and open receptivity. Allow yourself to drift off to sleep speaking your truth and embracing your power.

Journal

You may use this space or your own journal to write down any thoughts, feelings, ideas or insights that may have come up for you during the exercise.

DAY 22
SELF-EXPRESSION

Standing in Grace

Commentary

"Hollywood can't handle an Afro-centric King," I was told. "You have to uphold the King family legacy and look a certain way that is acceptable to all people." Well, I needed to be true to myself. I wanted no more chemicals in my hair. I wanted my hair to grow healthier and stronger. I wanted the natural beauty of my hair to shine forth. So, I decided to grow my hair into groomed dread locks. My decision caused much grief for people close to me. Locking your hair is not something you do overnight and change the next day. It requires a commitment. So needless to say, by the time I had arrived at the decision to do this, my mind was quite made up. So the negative comments and put-downs by loved ones went in one ear and out the other. I stood in grace, no need to argue, no need to convince, no need to even listen to petty concerns. When you are clear about something, grace happens. Hard to explain, but there is a sense of peace regardless of all else. Yes, I wanted to explain to them my decision so that they might find peace with it, but not because I needed to change their minds about anything. I just wanted them to be as free and as happy as I was—I was standing in grace.

Exercise

How to stand in grace with any situation.

1. Do your inner homework first—find **YOUR** truth. What feels right for you.
2. Make a sound decision based on your truth.
3. Commit to the decision you've made—don't allow yourself to waiver.
4. Stand by your decision—stand in grace with your head held high.

Do this process with everything you've been tentative on. The only way to embrace your power is to stand on solid ground and not be tentative or waiver about anything. Be clear and be free.

Affirmation

Commit the following positive affirmation to memory, and silently recite it to yourself throughout the day whenever you think of it, or to counter any negative thoughts, or to simply reinforce the idea that anything is possible in an abundant universe.

My life is grace unfolding.

Visualization

Pick a situation where you have waivered back and forward on making a decision. Now see that you have made one decision and you have decided to stick to it no matter what. See the end result of the decision you've made to be the best result you could have ever hoped for. Know that you are always guided and your decisions come from the deepest part of you, the part of you that is connected to an all-knowing God. Feel the blessings from the decision made. Be grateful for the decision, knowing it was the best decision and let go of any other alternatives—for you have decided. Notice how good it feels to have that decision behind you now. Feel free to move on with your life and comfortable making other decisions. Embrace your power by seeing yourself making clear decisions.

Journal

You may use this space or your own journal to write down any thoughts, feelings, ideas or insights that may have come up for you during the exercise.

DAY 23
SELF-EXPRESSION

How Well Am I Giving?

Commentary

My mind went blank when my assistant asked for a raise. Not that she didn't deserve it, not that I didn't have it to give. Blank because I thought we were happy with the way things were. She was a rather wise and generous soul, and when I hired her, she took a pay cut in order that I might put more money into the business. A year went by and she came to me saying she felt it was time to receive the amount offered at the time she was hired. Even though things were better financially, I struggled with the idea and asked her to compromise. Being the wise woman she was, her response was "I will do this if you like, but I don't want to support you in this limited thinking any longer." I gave her what she asked for. Within a few months, I found that I had indeed expanded my thinking and we were able to hire an additional assistant. I continue to watch when I open up and am not afraid to give—all of that which I give and more is returned to me. It is my prayer that your limited thinking is no longer supported by those around you.

Exercise

How well are you giving? Where have you wanted to give but were afraid to do so? For the next seven days your assignment is Fearless Giving! Know that you can't outgive God. So write down your Giving Plan for the next week. Give money to the homeless, if you have no money to give, give clothing, give food, give love, give smiles. Give everywhere you go! If you think you can't afford to give, you can't afford not to give, for this is the only way things will turn around for you. You must learn to be a good giver. Which means to give enthusiastically, be of good cheer! You will soon find that the more you give, the more powerful you become.

Affirmation

Commit the following positive affirmation to memory, and silently recite it to yourself throughout the day whenever you think of it, or to counter any negative thoughts, or to simply reinforce the idea that anything is possible in an abundant universe.

Giving is the gift of my soul's desire.

Visualization

See yourself as an extraordinary giver, a successful and happy philanthropist who loves giving and helping others. When you have self-mastery and have embraced your power, there is an automatic opening of overflow. It is from this place that you give. See it, believe it, give it away in order that you might be free to receive even more.

Journal

You may use this space or your own journal to write down any thoughts, feelings, ideas or insights that may have come up for you during the exercise.

DAY 24
SELF-EXPRESSION

Expressing My Magnificence

Commentary

The crowd roared with delight, wow, my very first standing ovation. I had been magnificent. I loved the recognition and appreciation for my work. I totally received it and took in the magnitude of applause. It was easy while I was on stage, still in character, and still in my comfort zone. However, off stage when people came up to me one-by-one and started telling me how magnificent I had been, I became totally embarrassed, not knowing what to say or how to respond. Why do we shy away when being confronted with praise? Because we are not empowered enough to handle it. And because we can't handle the praise, we often choose not to express our magnificence.

Today, I am empowered enough to receive my compliments with grace, because I now realize that it is the God within others that is recognizing the God within me. And I give thanks for this. In order for me to accept my magnificence, I had to first realize that I was a child of God, and that there are no mistakes in God. God is magnificent and God created me. I am a magnificent work of art. And, there is something that God has placed inside of me that is magnificent and seeks expression out into the world. My soul's urge is to express its magnificence. This is THE reason I was born. This is the reason you were born—to express your magnificence! Once we understand that it is the God within us that is magnificent, we can enjoy being told good things about ourselves. And, it is our duty to share the magnificence within us that God has so blessed us to carry.

Exercise

Stand up, legs apart and arms stretched up and out to the sky, recognizing this abundant universe we live in. Imagine yourself standing before the vast ocean, and feel the incredible energy of the universe rushing through you as you breathe in and out deeply. Take a deep breath in and say out loud, "I am willing to be more than I've ever been before." Release the breath. Breathe in slowly and deeply saying, " I surrender to my magnificence, allowing it to carry me where my soul wants to go." Release the breath. Breathe in deeply again saying, "I surrender, I trust, I am."

Note: Do this exercise now, and again the next time you find yourself at the ocean facing the massive body of water, the liquid essence of God. Make it more powerful, shout it out—allowing it to sink deep into every cell of your being. This is really a beautiful exercise at sunrise or sunset.

Affirmation

Commit the following positive affirmation to memory, and silently recite it to yourself throughout the day whenever you think of it, or to counter any negative thoughts, or to simply reinforce the idea that anything is possible in an abundant universe.

I am releasing my magnificence now!

Visualization

Going back to today's exercise, see yourself standing before the ocean, knowing that this very large body of water is the liquid creative essence of God. Knowing that you are a part of the ocean, as all of life started in the ocean. Knowing that the ocean is a part of you, as your body is made up of mostly water. Begin to feel your essence merging with the ocean waters, merging with the essence of God. Feel and sense the magnificence of God moving through you, through your entire body. Feel just how magnificent you truly are. Feel how powerful you truly are. Now see yourself doing what you love to do, pursuing your dreams, living out your mission, releasing and channeling your magnificence in such a way that the whole world knows you have arrived. Carry this vision and this feeling with you into your dream state tonight and remember, it's your life you are creating, so dream big.

Journal

You may use this space or your own journal to write down any thoughts, feelings, ideas or insights that may have come up for you during the exercise.

Self-Appreciation
Steps 25 through 28

Embracing Your Power

*Once we express ourselves authentically,
we tend to feel so vulnerable
that it is easy to give up our power if the expression
is not well received. So we must be able to acknowledge
and appreciate ourselves for expressing
who we are and not allow others to diminish our expressions
with their personal judgments and opinions.*

DAY 25
SELF-APPRECIATION

No Need For Approval

Commentary

"Yoki, actors have a hard time making a living. I just want you to have a good life." My father was a logical man, and even though he believed in me, he still doubted my decision to want to become an actor. Because of our close connection, I desperately needed his approval. I believe that most of us are forever seeking the approval of our mother or father or both. Somehow, it just seems very difficult to cut the ties so that we are individuals standing on our own, standing in our own power, and not needing the approval of one or both of our parents. My wanting to become an actor was not comfortable for my father which made me feel like I was making a poor choice. I began doubting myself and making choices that were not in alignment with my soul. They were off target because I was aiming for his approval. I had to learn to accept that if I was going to be happy, I needed to do what was right for me, even though it may not have seemed right to my father.

We are all children of God with a special mission in life. If we follow the dreams of others, we will miss out on fulfilling our mission. We will arrive at the end of our lives with all of our gifts still stuffed inside, dying with us. I want to leave this world with no regrets, knowing I have released all of my gifts unto the world. To do this, I can't wait for approval from anyone. I have to be true to myself and live my life without the need for approval from anyone.

Exercise

Sometimes when we don't receive the approval we seek, we either try harder or give up completely. Take a look at your life and see if there are any areas where you find yourself trying too hard to get approval. Or, see if there are areas in your life where you have given up and have acquired the "I don't care" attitude. In order to embrace your power, you must be willing to release the need for approval. So look at these areas where you have given your power away to another in search of their approval, and write a letter. The letter is to you from God, and God is telling you how much you are loved and that YOU are enough. Write the letter to you from God now. Allow your mind to be open and receive the blessings of this letter which will release you from any need to seek approval from anyone outside of yourself. YOU ARE ENOUGH just the way you are.

Affirmation

Commit the following positive affirmation to memory, and silently recite it to yourself throughout the day whenever you think of it, or to counter any negative thoughts, or to simply reinforce the idea that anything is possible in an abundant universe.

The core of my being delights in the presence that I Am.

(Don't analyze it, just feel its resonance as you say it.)

Visualization

See a pile of paperwork before you. These papers document your life up to this point. No matter what mistakes you've made, you realize it is all about learning, growing and evolving. So you've learned not to judge yourself, to be kind to yourself, to love yourself, no matter what. Next to this pile of documents is a very large rubber stamp that says "APPROVED" in bright red ink.

As you drift off to sleep tonight, see yourself stamping each document of your life being stamped with the word "APPROVED."

Journal

You may use this space or your own journal to write down any thoughts, feelings, ideas or insights that may have come up for you during the exercise.

DAY 26
SELF-APPRECIATION

No Need To Be Needed

Commentary

$10,000.00 in credit card debt. Not mine. But I had to pay the bill. Why, because I was helping a friend. Loaned my car out. It's stolen and totaled. Once again, I pay the price for helping a friend. I needed to be needed in order to feel good about myself. It made me feel good to realize that people needed me and could count on me to help them out. Needing to be needed can cause havoc in your life if you're not careful. Rescuing a friend is okay every now and then, however, when you find that you must rescue someone in order to feel good about yourself, you are out of balance. I always had somebody in my life that needed rescuing, somebody to fulfill my need. I would use compassion as protection. The more compassion I would have for these poor souls, the more assured I was that they would stay in my life and continue to fulfill the need that I had to be needed. When we embrace our power, we have the power to say "no" and to recognize when saying "no" is important to our own well-being. If helping others has become your hobby and it makes you feel important, you might ask yourself, "what am I doing to empower my own life?" As I became more and more empowered, I began to know when it was right for me to help someone and when it was best for me to pray and stay out of the way.

Exercise

Questions to Ponder

- Is there anyone in your life that constantly calls upon you for help?
- Do you fuss about it, but deep within you are you glad they called upon you?
- Do you feel like if you don't help then nobody else will, like you are their only hope?
- If so, do you realize how arrogant you are and how limited your faith in God is?

Decide now to release them, and let God be in charge of them. Step out of the way and let go. Make a conscious choice to draw healthy people into your life so that you may become more healthy. I am not saying you have to release unhealthy people, particularly if they are your loved ones, but you should recognize how you are serving each other's weaknesses. Begin to establish a new model for your relationship.

Affirmation

Commit the following positive affirmation to memory, and silently recite it to yourself throughout the day whenever you think of it, or to counter any negative thoughts, or to simply reinforce the idea that anything is possible in an abundant universe.

I no longer need to be needed;
I shine sufficiently unto myself.

Visualization

Pick an individual you have been helping, someone you know you need to stop helping as s/he has become dependent upon you, tying you to him/her and stifling the both of you. See this person surrounded by a pink bubble—pink is the color of universal love. See them laughing and playing and celebrating in this bubble of love. Now see that there are very large hands around this bubble, the hands of God. Know now, as you drift off to sleep that they are being taken care of as you have released them to God, and you are no longer in charge of their well being. Know that the next time s/he ask you for help, you must say no in order to stay out of God's way. God has many helpers and many ways of helping. Sometimes it looks like a painful path, but it is always the right path when we let go and let God.

Journal

You may use this space or your own journal to write down any thoughts, feelings, ideas or insights that may have come up for you during the exercise.

DAY 27
SELF-APPRECIATION

No Need to Be Acknowledged

Commentary

I love being recognized and acknowledged for doing good work—we all do. It is one thing to appreciate the recognition and acknowledgment, it is another thing to "need" it. When you can do something simply for the love of doing it, then you have embraced your power. You see, the gift is truly in the giving. When you are looking for the gift in the end result, you miss it all together. When the end comes and you are acknowledged for doing something wonderful, that should simply be icing on the cake. Doing the work should have been your cake, your absolute joy. Needing approval is needing another to be okay with who you are or what you are doing. Needing to be acknowledged is needing another to recognize and validate who you are or what you are doing. To embrace your power, you must know that you don't need approval or recognition, even though both feel really good. You only need to know that you are enough, and when you do your best, that is enough as well.

Exercise

Make a list of all the things you can think of where you feel you didn't receive the acknowledgment you deserved. Now meditate on each item and identify what you did receive from the experience. Did you receive any joy or personal rewards whatsoever? If not, let this be a lesson to stand in your power in the future; only doing those things which bring YOU joy. If you did receive personal gratification, allow that to be all that you need. If the acknowledgment has to come from someone else, you've given away your power again. Take back your power by acknowledging yourself for a job well done.

Affirmation

Commit the following positive affirmation to memory, and silently recite it to yourself throughout the day whenever you think of it, or to counter any negative thoughts, or to simply reinforce the idea that anything is possible in an abundant universe.

I acknowledge and celebrate the light that I am.

Visualization

Bring to mind the last time you saw someone and they failed to say hello or acknowledge you. How did that make you feel? Think of the last time you did something really wonderful, and you didn't get the recognition you thought you deserved. How did that make you feel?

Now go back to each situation and change it. See that person who failed to greet you passing you by. Imagine yourself smiling as they pass, for you have incorporated in your heart that if a person does not have a smile, you give them one of yours. Recall that wonderful thing you did for someone and they failed to acknowledge you for it. See yourself smiling and living in joy simply because you've learned that in order to grow, you must release life's energy so you do for others with a cheerful heart, expecting nothing in return. You have learned to be of good cheer, regardless of circumstance. See yourself smiling and feel your heart smiling as you drift off to sleep, knowing that life is good—very good.

Journal

You may use this space or your own journal to write down any thoughts, feelings, ideas or insights that may have come up for you during the exercise.

DAY 28
SELF-APPRECIATION

Celebrating My Life

Commentary

Have you ever just wanted out? Out of the body, off of the planet? Live long enough and you will experience a dark night of the soul, where you just want out. Well, I've gone through a few and what I learned to do to get back on track was to just appreciate life. Do you have any idea about the miracle of "You?" The entire Universe had to be in sync in order for you to come into existence as you are. Everything has to be working in perfect harmony in order for you to continue to exist. You may look around you and see disorder and chaos. You may look around you and see war and poverty, sickness, and violence. But you must realize there is a master plan at work, and we are all part of it. You have to know that there are no mistakes in God. You are not a mistake. You are a miracle, and if you are to embrace your power, you must begin to celebrate your life. You must see your life as the life of God. You must know that your life has purpose, direction, and importance. You have unique gifts to give that only you can give. Once you begin to appreciate your very life, then you can live in celebration of who you are. Your gifts will start to unfold, and you won't be able to stop them. As you embrace your power, you will start living life more fully, more completely, more passionately, and the dark night of the soul will become a thing of the past. If you don't make a big fuss over your birthday, start! It is the day you showed up and should be celebrated. If you do celebrate, extend the celebration throughout the entire year so that you are celebrating your life, each and every day you are alive.

Exercise

Design a plan to celebrate your life. You would not start building a house without a plan. You would not do anything important without a strategy. It's time you created a plan to celebrate your life. Decide to do something wonderful for you more than once a year on your birthday. Decide that every day is a new/birth day and celebrate. From this day forward, ask yourself each morning upon rising, "How will I celebrate my life today?" Never let a day go by without celebrating your life. If you celebrate your life every day, there won't be a day that goes by where you will allow anyone to take away your power by dishonoring you or crossing your boundaries. You will know that your life is too important—you will always embrace your power!

Affirmation

Commit the following positive affirmation to memory, and silently recite it to yourself throughout the day whenever you think of it, or to counter any negative thoughts, or to simply reinforce the idea that anything is possible in an abundant universe.

Today I celebrate the gift that I am.

Visualization

What makes you feel good? What can you do for yourself that brings you sheer delight? See yourself pampering yourself, soaking in a warm bubble bath, getting a massage, meditating, writing in your journal, reading a good book, watching a wonderful movie, singing your song before thousands of people, performing, dancing. Whatever makes you feel good about life, see yourself engaged in that activity.

Allow the feelings this activity generates within you to expand throughout your entire being as you drift off to sleep. Celebrate your life through all of eternity.

Journal

You may use this space or your own journal to write down any thoughts, feelings, ideas or insights that may have come up for you during the exercise.

Self-Mastery

Steps 29 through 30

Living In the Love

DAY 29
SELF-MASTERY

Transcending Pain

Commentary

Excruciating pain for 2 solid days. Day 3 and the pain continues. Embracing your power somehow seems harder to do when you find your body in pain. I went to the dentist to have a couple of wisdom teeth pulled, and the healing process wasn't as easy as I would have liked it to be. I ended up in excruciating pain for days and it would not go away. Every time I would eat something, the pain would strike and almost bring me to my knees. And it would not go away. Pain killers didn't work, and the dentist wasn't available until days later. So I had to learn to transcend the pain. I could have given my power away to the pain and allow it to dictate my life. But no, I embraced my power. I dealt with the pain and got on with my life. Pain is inevitable, suffering is a choice. I chose not to suffer. For three days I went about my daily activities in pain but with the spirit of joy. I refused to suffer and allow the pain, to get the best of me. We must learn to embrace our power, even in the face of pain. This is truly self-mastery.

Exercise

Physical pain is a signal to let you know something needs attention. It is not a signal to lie down and die. You find out the cause of the pain and you do what you can to take care of the problem. Once you've done all that you can do, shift your focus away from the pain, and channel your energy into a project or something else to keep your mind occupied and thinking different thoughts. To master pain is a bonus point for embracing your power. You must redirect your thoughts and be in control of your mind to hold onto your power.

Affirmation

Commit the following positive affirmation to memory, and silently recite it to yourself throughout the day whenever you think of it, or to counter any negative thoughts, or to simply reinforce the idea that anything is possible in an abundant universe.

My body is healed by the renewing of my mind.

Visualization

If you are experiencing pain in your body, see that part of your body filled with and surrounded by sparkling particles of white light, like golden fairy dusk. You can amplify the experience by placing your hand over that part of the body as we all have healing hands that radiate energy. Where there is dis-ease, there is always a lack of energy flowing to that part, so using your focused awareness, visualize sending more energy or white light directly to that weakened part of the body. Just see the light circulating in, out, through, and around that area. Then see the light change from white to blue, a calming feeling, then from blue to green, a very healing vibration. You can send the energy and play with the dancing lights as you drift off to sleep. If you play with this visualization long enough, allowing it to hold your attention, even the pain won't keep you awake. It will surrender as you embrace your power and drift into a nice peaceful sleep. Sleep well.

Journal

You may use this space or your own journal to write down any thoughts, feelings, ideas or insights that may have come up for you during the exercise.

DAY 30
SELF-MASTERY

Falling In Love

Commentary

Oh, he was so fine! I had to pinch myself to make sure I wasn't dreaming. He was real, and I just knew that he was the mate I had been praying for. I had been looking around every corner. And then one day, he showed up. Not only did he show up and seem perfect for me, but he showed up looking ever so fine. I just knew this was the man God had sent to be my husband, so my mind started racing towards the altar. I did everything in my power to slow down my thoughts, but nothing could stop them. These particular thoughts had been at bay far too long—they were out of control.

As I started to share some of my thoughts with him, he let me know right away that I was moving too fast. He said I was on page 108, and he was still on page 8. I was crushed. I had fallen in love, and was completely out of control. I believe this man was sent to teach me how to step into love gracefully. What does it mean to step into love rather than to "fall" in love? It means to hold onto your power so that you don't lose yourself in the relationship. This is truly a lesson in self-mastery. If you can transcend pain and not lose yourself when you fall in love, you will never have to worry about not being in your power again. You are truly an empowered being taking life by the horns.

Exercise

If you find you are "falling" in love, start to pull back just a little to get a hold of yourself. Pulling back does not have to mean physical distance, but it does mean emotional distance. Pull back far enough to become the observer of yourself and your reactions. You will know when you are falling because there is a sensation of being out of control. When you start to feel this sensation, remind yourself that falling is painful and decide to stand firmly, stand strong so that you can take it slowly, step by step, stepping into love more gracefully. When you fall, usually one person will fall faster than the other. When you take steps, you are usually stepping together. Recite your affirmation continually as a mantra to help you remain emotionally stable. Distract your thoughts and focus on your spiritual practices to keep your mind on the right track. Watch your words. Try not to say things like "I love you" or "I need you" or "I miss you" too soon. Keep your language just beyond friendly when you are teasing and playful. Don't get serious too quickly or you will fall, and you will most likely frighten your partner away.

Affirmation

Commit the following positive affirmation to memory, and silently recite it to yourself throughout the day whenever you think of it, or to counter any negative thoughts, or to simply reinforce the idea that anything is possible in an abundant universe.

*I am totally willing and able
to STEP into love gracefully.*

Visualization

See yourself standing before a large pond of water. See this water turn beautiful shades of pink colors, the color of universal love. Now watch yourself slowly walk into the water, allowing yourself to be emerged into the pool of love. Stepping into love ever so slowly, ever so gracefully. Feel the moisture of the water caressing your feet, your ankles, your legs. As you step deeper and deeper into love, know that you are safe and in full control. Know that you can take a step back anytime you feel the need. But for now, see yourself progress ever so slowly, stepping into love ever so gracefully as you drift off to sleep. This is what it feels like to know love surrounds you, carries you. Love is everywhere you are.

Journal

You may use this space or your own journal to write down any thoughts, feelings, ideas or insights that may have come up for you during the exercise.

Yolanda King

Speaker, Actor, Producer

Yolanda King (Los Angeles, CA) is an internationally rec-ognized motivational speaker and actor. Yolanda's mission is to encourage personal and social change through her artistic endeavors, including writing, acting, producing, speaking, and teaching.

Born in Montgomery, Alabama, Yolanda is the first born child of Coretta Scott King and Dr. Martin Luther King, Jr., and has been in the midst of the quest for human rights and peace all of her life. She has performed or lectured in 49 of the 50 American states as well as in Europe, Africa, and Asia for edu-cational, business, religious, and civic organizations. Sharing her message of the importance of embracing our common human-ity, Yolanda has sounded the call from the halls of the United Nations to venues in Moscow and Munich. Yolanda King has been acclaimed for her ability to inspire people to reach higher ground, to motivate people to move forward, and to empower people to make a difference.

As a seasoned and respected actor, many of Ms. King's stage, television, and film credits reflect her commitment to personal and social change and include portrayals of Rosa Parks in the NBC-TV movie "King," Dr. Betty Shabazz in the film, "Death of a Prophet" with Morgan Freeman, and Medgar Ever's daugh-ter, Reena, in "Ghosts of Mississippi." Focusing on the highlights of the Civil Rights Movement, Yolanda King's most recent theatrical production "Achieving the Dream," in which she portrays several characters, is a product of her unique relationship with her father, and her deep insight into this pivotal time in our history.

Ms. King has been honored with numerous presentations, awards, and citations by organizations around the world and has been named one of the Outstanding Young Women of America.

For Speaking Engagements and Performances
Contact Higher Ground Productions, Inc.
1-323-295-4144
www.Yolanda-King.com

Wanda Marie

Personal Development Trainer / Consultant

I do more than help my clients to achieve their goals, I help them to develop a whole new way of being. My clients learn to set healthy boundaries based on their true values, to acknowledge their needs and learn to stop chasing them, and start getting them met, to believe in the possibility of their dreams, to stop doing ideas and start doing what's meaningful, to say "no" when they need to, to receive with ease and without guilt, to let go with grace, to live life fully, to give up toxic relationships, and foster self-love, and to commit to success one day at a time.

Moving beyond comfort zones requires adequate desire, belief, courage, and dedication to a specific outcome. I am committed to providing an avenue for individuals and groups to expand these qualities within themselves by gently moving them from a place of feeling stuck to a path of focus, direction and power. Simply, I'm in the business of transforming lives through values based counseling, coaching, and training programs.

I've been on this path for more than twenty years and have created numerous programs that have assisted hundreds of individuals in leading richer more meaningful lives. My most current project has been the development of the Personal Freedom Program on behalf of Yolanda King and Higher

Ground Productions. This program is a holistic learning system, developed from my twenty years of work in the field of personal development and human potential. The Program combines the practical with the spiritual for a complete, holistic learning-experience. This Program is designed to help people to move beyond surviving and start thriving.

You are invited to visit my Website at www.WandaMarie.com or phone me directly at (310) 827-4166.

www.WandaMarie.com

INDEX OF
DAILY POSITIVE AFFIRMATIONS

1. I am divinity expressing life fully.
2. I know who I am and my purpose reveals itself clearly.
3. Obstacles are merely open doors for my magnificence to shine through.
4. I enjoy the freedom of moving forward.
5. My mind is the mind of infinite intelligence.
6. I adore the me that I have become.
7. My body reflects the beauty of my inner thoughts.
8. I have supreme love for all that I am.
9. I release the past freeing myself and everyone else.
10. I am in love with the me that I am becoming.
11. My boundaries are clear, honored, and respected by all.
12. Playing creates more prosperity by freeing up my creative energy.
13. I release the past and fully embrace all of my power now.
14. All that I need is added unto me now.
15. My life is sacred and precious as I am a child of the Most High.
16. Within the stillness, I am whole.
17. The success I create is my faith in action.
18. My positive focus redefines my state of being.
19. I stand tall and secure in who I am.
20. My faith expands day by day.
21. My truth is spoken with love and integrity.
22. My life is grace unfolding.

23. Giving is the gift of my soul's desire.
24. I am releasing my magnificence now!
25. The core of my being delights in the presence that I Am.
26. I no longer need to be needed; I shine sufficiently unto myself.
27. I acknowledge and celebrate the light that I am.
28. Today I celebrate the gift that I am.
29. My body is healed by the renewing of my mind.
30. I am totally willing and able to STEP into love gracefully.